Dukan Diet Cookbook

45 Simple and Delicious Attack Phase Recipes for the Dukan Diet Weight Loss Plan

Sydney Rush

Table of Contents

Turkey Shirataki

Caraway Flavored Pork Chops

Oat Bran Galette Sandwich

Dukan Beef Tataki

Oriental Style Braised Beef

Egg and Onion Bhurji

Salmon in Wasabi Sauce

Turkey Meatloaf

Lemon Zesty Grilled Calamari with Garlic

Pan Fried Trout with Lemon & Bay Leaf

Snacks & Appetizers

Cinnamon Oat Bran Muffins

Israeli-Spiced Meatballs

Dukan Coffee Frappuccino

Herb-Sauteed Shrimp

Meatball Stuffed Mushrooms

Chicken Breast Wrapped in Turkey Bacon

Stuffed Eggs with Shrimps/Prawns

Dukan Prawn Cocktail

Winter Warming Eggnog

Oat Bran Free Dukan Diet Rolls

Why Dukan?

People often consider a diet as a phase – something to help you get to your goal weight, but not a lasting lifestyle change. Then, once they've lost the weight, they go back to how they were eating before and gain it all back. The Dukan Diet takes this into consideration and plans to help followers of the diet maintain a healthy weight for years to come.

The Dukan Diet consists of four phases. The first two phases are for weight loss, and the second two are for maintaining your True Weight, which is your ideal weight determined by your height, age, current weight, gender, and weight history. With Dukan, acheiving your goal is possible, and you don't have to do it alone.

Here are the four phases of the Dukan Diet:

1) Attack Phase

Many followers of the Dukan Diet find themselves shedding the pounds like crazy in the first phase. Don't be surprised if you lose a jean size in the first week!

Depending on the amount of weight you need to use, the Attack Phase can last from 1 to 7 days, but it is usually around 2 to 5 days. In this phase, only foods on the Pure Protein list are allowed. The list consists of lean red meat, poultry, seafood, soy, fat-free dairy products, and eggs. Shirataki, a Japanese root vegetable that is often made into a carb-free pasta, is also allowed, as well as a limited amounts of goji berries and oat bran. The catch: you can eat as much as you want! No restrictions whatsoever as long as you stay on the allowed food list.

During this time, you will experience ketosis, so it is important to drink 6 to 8 glasses of water per day to allow the ketones to flush from your body. It is also essential to exercise daily, preferably in the morning, to experience maximum weight loss.

2) Cruise Phase

The Cruise Phase varies greatly in length depending on the amount of weight you need to lose. In this phase, you will alternate between Pure Protein days and Protein and Vegetable days. On Protein and Vegetable days, only non-starchy vegetables from the 100 Allowed Food list can be eaten. These veggies include cauliflower, asparagus, broccoli, carrots, onions, tomatoes, and zucchini. In the Cruise Phase, 1 teaspoon of olive oil is allowed as well.

Dukan recommends 30 minutes of brisk walking per day in the Cruise Phase to optimize weight loss. That's less than the length of one television programme!

3) Consolidation Phase

The Consolidation Phase begins after you have achieved your weight loss goal. It lasts 5 days for every pound lost. It will gradually add to your meal plan to form healthy eating habits that will last you the rest of your life. If you find you have trouble keeping weight off once you've lost it, Dukan is the plan for you.

In the first half of this phase, you will be allowed a serving of fruit every day, 2 slices of whole grain bread per day, 1.5 ounces of hard rind cheese daily, 1 cup of starchy foods per week, and 1 celebration meal per week, which includes an appetizer, entree, dessert, and a glass of wine.

In the second half of the Consolidation phase, the serving of fruit is increased to two per day and you are allowed 2 servings of starchy foods and 2 celebration meals per week.

As part of this phase, one day per week is set aside as a Pure Protein day, and brisk walking for 30 minutes per day must be maintained. These healthy habits will be a foundation to keep you at your True Weight for the rest of your life!

4) Stabilization Phase

This phase will last you the rest of your life and keep you from going back to old habits that will make you regain the weight you've lost.

During this phase, there are only three non-negotiable rules: eat 3 tablespoons of oat bran per day, take the stairs whenever possible, have one Pure Protein day per week.

Because protein is a big part of the Dukan Diet diet, you will feel fuller longer and crave fewer snacks during the day, leading to weight loss. Protein is complex, meaning it takes longer to digest and does not spike the blood sugar, leading to a crash. Protein is also essential to building muscle, so those who are trying to gain muscle mass will see increased progress on the Dukan Diet. Diabetics also see improvements in sustaining regular blood-sugar levels.

Meat and fish are also excellent sources of Omega-3 fatty acids, which aid in brain function, circulation, and promote healthy hair, skin, and nails. You will often find your brain function improved with an increase in these fats. Olive oil often used beginning in the cruise phase as an alternative to vegetable oil, which is made from soy beans, or peanut oil. They can also help reduce risk of stroke, improve cases of inflammatory diseases such as rheumatoid arthritis, and may aid in mental disorders such as depression and dementia.

Many opponents of the Dukan Diet cite the high meat intake as a concern related to kidney function, but the Dukan Diet diet actually balances dietary acids in the kidneys better than the traditional diet. Grains and meat increase acids in the kidneys, whereas vegetables yield alkaline pH in the kidneys. Because the Dukan Diet diet encourages more veggies and fewer grains, this balances the increased amount of meat in the diet and helps improve kidney function and reduces cases of gout.

The Dukan Diet diet also decreases disorders and conditions related to sugar because it excludes processed sugar, dairy, and carbohydrates that convert to sugar in the body. Most followers of Dukan Diet notice a decrease in skin conditions like acne, psoriasis, and rosacea that can be caused by sugar and dairy. Dukan Diet can also improve Type II Diabetes by decreasing intake of foods that require insulin to break down.

The Dukan Diet diet also leads to an increase in vitamins A, C, B12, and Potassium intake, because none of these vitamins are present in grains in a form that can be absorbed by the body. The beneficial substances supplied by grains and dairy in a normal diet include iron, fiber, calcium, vitamin D, and thiamine, all of which can be found in the Dukan Diet diet. Iron is present in dark, leafy greens in higher rates than in grains. It can also be found in beef, pork, many goji berries, poultry, and fish. Fiber is very prevalent in non-starchy veggies and fruits. Seafood and leafy veggies contain calcium, and thiamine is present in asparagus, kale, cauliflower, and eggs.

Not only will you lose weight, but you'll be healthier on the Dukan Diet! All of these increased vitamins and more physical activity will help you stay fit and look good for years to come!

It may seem like a big undertaking to start the Dukan Diet, but with the creative and indulgent recipes listed in a few pages, you'll notice that you won't be missing a thing – and you'll be enjoying a fitter body and a healthier life.

Food to Avoid

You will want to avoid:

Grains: Bread, cereal, oatmeal, and rice are all forbidden on the Dukan Diet. Grains are calorie-dense, easy to digest, and lack vitamins. Because they are so easy to digest, our body does so quickly, causing our blood sugar to rise sharply. This is why carbs are a source of quick energy, but what happens next will often result in an unhealthy energy crash. After the blood sugar spikes, our bodies will then respond by quickly producing the hormone insulin to help digest the carbs. This results in a low feeling, mental fogginess, and lack of fullness, causing us to eat more to feel full again. On the Dukan Diet, the protein and fiber-dense foods will keep you fuller longer, meaning you will have no need to count calories to make sure you don't overeat. Instead, you can use the allowed oat bran, zero calorie sweetener, and egg recipes to make muffins, pancakes, and other treats should you get a craving for carbs.

Processed Foods and Beverages: Dukan Diet excludes processed foods and drinks, which eliminates unhealthy preservatives from the diet. Pre-made or frozen meals often contain added sugar or salt for flavor, so eliminating them from the diet is beneficial for the heart and will result in weight loss. Even processed foods that seem healthy, like juice, are filled with extra sugar and contain none of the filling fiber of whole, raw fruit. There is just no way to know what has been added into frozen TV dinners. When you are on the Dukan

Diet, you will eat only whole, natural foods that you can list all the ingredients to.

Dairy: Many people don't realize it, but dairy is packed with fat and sugars. Dairy can often cause breakouts or digestive problems in adults, so reducing or eliminating it from the diet can result in healthier skin and more regular digestion. With the Dukan Diet, low or no fat dairy that is low in sugar is okay in moderation.

Fruit: The Dukan Diet also excludes fruit in the first two phases. While it is true that fruit contains fiber and vitamins, they don't have anything that can't be found in the vegetables and goji berries on the allowed foods list. Goji berries are rich in 11 different kinds of vitamins, and many of the vegetables on the list such as kale, spinach, and celery are packed with fiber. Like protein, fiber is a dense food that will keep you full longer and reduce cravings.

Sweets: Of course, the Dukan Diet eliminates sweets like cookies and chocolate in the first two phases as these items are calorie dense, fatty, and have no nutritional value. However, you are still able to eat many delicious concoctions that involve oat bran and eggs, a surprisingly delicious combination. Don't worry, you'll will be able to eat regular sweets again too in the final two phases.

Alcohol: Alcohol turns to sugar in the body aand provides no nourishment, so it is forbidden in the Attack and Cruise Phases.

Attack Phase Recipes

Take a look at the next section, which contains delicious recipes from rich and hearty fillets to desserts to tasty breakfast ideas that you can eat during the attack phase. Remember, the attack phase consists of only protein, oat bran, and shirataki noodles. If you think you can't get through the first two phases without your favorite foods, the following recipes will definitely change your mind. There are even a few tasty beverages that will tantalize your taste buds and leave you without feeling deprived.

Breakfast

Filet Mignon Scramble

Prep time: 10 min

Cook time: Approx. 20 min

Servings: 1

INGREDIENTS

1 8 oz filet mignon

2 cups egg white substitute (or 8 eggs)

1/2 cup fat free sour cream

1/4 cup chives, chopped

1/4 cup fat free milk

cooking spray

salt and pepper

INSTRUCTIONS

1. Sear filet in a sauté pan for 5 minutes on each side. Set aside and allow to cool. Slice into thin strips on cool.
2. Turn heat to low and add egg mixture to sauté pan. Cook for about 5 minutes.
3. Add filet slices right before removing from heat
4. Serve with sour cream and chives.

Dukan Muffins

Prep time: 5 min

Cook time: Approx. 20 min

Servings: 1 (Yield 12 muffins)

INGREDIENTS

6 Tbsp. Oat bran

6 Tbsp. Wheat bran

3 Tbsp. Fromage frais

3 Tbsp. Sweetener

3 Tbsp. Cherry low fat yogurt

1 tsp Baking powder

Dash Nutmeg

Dash Skimmed milk

Spray oil low calorie

INSTRUCTIONS

1. Preheat oven to 200C or gas mark 6.
2. Mix together all ingredients except for spray oil. Blend together until mixture is smooth with no bumps in batter.
3. Spoon mixture into muffin liners (yield at 12 muffins).

4. Bake for 10 minutes or until golden brown. Serve with sweetener.

Eggs Cocotte

Prep time: 10 min

Cook time: Approx. 5 min

Servings: 1 (Yield 3 ramekins)

INGREDIENTS
3 eggs
1 slices of smoked salmon (ham or bresaola)
6 tsp virtually fat-free fromage frais
Tarragon (or chervil), chopped
Salt and black pepper

INSTRUCTIONS
1. Put water in a high sided sauce pan (like a bain-marie) to boil.
2. In three ramekin dishes add 2 tsp of the fromage frais. And a dash of herbs in each.
3. Cut smoked salmon (or meat of choice) into fine strips.
4. Split the salmon into 3, adding each piece into a ramekin with salt and pepper and one egg each.
5. In boiling water, add ramekins. Over medium heat, cook covered for 3–5 minutes.

Goji Berry Jam

Prep time: 5 min

Cook time: Approx. 40 min

Servings: 1

INGREDIENTS

5 Tbsp. Dukan Diet Goji Berries

3 scoops Dukan Diet Organic Stevia or to taste

1 tsp of Lemon Juice

1 tsp Agar-agar

Water (to cover the berries)

INSTRUCTIONS

1. Add Goji berries in a small non-stick saucepan. Add water and soak for 30 minutes.
2. Put in the lemon juice and stevia. Stirring constantly, bring to a boil.
3. Continue to stir the contents, add in the agar-agar. Cook for 7 or 8 minutes.
4. Put your finished jam into a glass jar. Refrigerate. Jam will keep for 4 days.

Indian Spicy Omelet

Prep time: 10 min

Cook time: Approx. 5 min

Servings: 1

INGREDIENTS

2 eggs

Half a green chilli, de-seeded and chopped into small bits

Half a red onion, finely chopped

1 spring onion, finely sliced

1 Tbsp. fresh coriander, chopped

A pinch of garam masala

A pinch of turmeric

Salt and pepper

INSTRUCTIONS

1. In a bowl mix eggs, salt, and pepper. Mixing gently with a fork to blend yolks and whites.
2. Add the chili, onion, spring onion, coriander and spices to the mix and combine with the eggs.

3. Lightly grease a non-stick pan with olive oil and heat to medium heat.

4. Pour the egg mixture into the pan and let it cook on one side for a couple of minutes. Flip to other side to finish cooking. Serve immediately.

Bacon and Scrambled Egg Sandwich

Prep time: 15 min

Cook time: Approx. 25 min

Servings: 2

INGREDIENTS

1 pack of turkey bacon rashers

4 eggs

2 oat bran galettes

4 Tbsp. skimmed milk

A pinch of dried dill

Salt and pepper

INSTRUCTIONS

1. Prepare two pancakes using the oat bran galette basic recipe, set aside on a plate and cover with foil to keep them warm

2. To make the scrambled eggs, Mix 4 eggs and skimmed milk until well blended. Add salt and pepper and a dash of dried dill (or chives or tarragon if preferred).

3. Heat a non-stick pan with spray oil over medium heat. Put in egg mixture until slightly set. Using a rubber

spatula and scrape the sides of pan and move them into the middle of the pan. Keep folding the eggs into the middle until done but still moist.

4. In a second non-stick skillet, spray with vegetable spray, heat over a medium heat to fry the turkey rashers.

5. Place cooked rashers over the pancakes,add scrambled eggs on top Then add in the oat bran galettes to create two sandwiches. Serve hot.

Sweet Oat Bran Galette With Toffee Yogurt

Prep time: 10 min

Cook time: Approx. 15 min

Servings: 1

INGREDIENTS

1 egg

2 Tbsp. oat bran

2 Tbsp. 0% fat greek yogurt

1 tsp sweetener

1 small pot of low fat toffee yogurt

INSTRUCTIONS

1. Whisk together the egg, oat bran, yogurt and sweetener until you obtain a smooth batter.
2. Lightly grease a non-stick pan and heat up to medium heat.
3. Pour in half of the mixture and cook the pancake on both sites until golden brown. Then transfer to a plate

and cover with tin foil to keep warm. Repeat step 2 to prepare the second pancake.

4. Serve with the toffee yogurt or any other flavored low fat yogurt, such as vanilla.

Smoked Salmon And Cream Cheese Wrap

Prep time: 10 min

Cook time: Approx. 15 min

Servings: 2

INGREDIENTS

A few slices of good quality smoked salmon

1 chive flavored oat bran galette

1 Tbsp. low fat cream cheese

Black pepper

INSTRUCTIONS

1. Use our basic recipe for the oat bran galette and add a tablespoon of fresh chopped chives to the batter before pouring the mix into the pan.
2. Once the pancake is ready, let it cool down on a plate for a couple of minutes. If the pancake is still hot it might crack when you start preparing the wrap.

3. Spread the cream cheese on the galette, place the smoked salmon on top and season with black pepper.

4. To fold the wrap, fold in the sides of the pancake and then roll from the bottom up. Cut the wrap in half and serve.

Vanilla Oat Bran Porridge

Prep time: 15 min

Cook time: Approx. 15 min

Servings: 1

INGREDIENTS

3 Tbsp. oat bran

125 ml of skim or zero fat milk.

Vanilla essence to taste

Sweetener to taste

INSTRUCTIONS

1. Put the milk and oat bran in a microwaveable safe bowl. Heat on high for 45 seconds.
2. Take out of microwave and add the vanilla and sweetener to taste.
3. Allow oat bran to stand, to soak up the milk.
4. Cook in microwave 45 seconds longer. Serve hot.

Plain Tofu Soufflé

Prep time: 10 min

Cook time: Approx. 25 min

Servings: 1

INGREDIENTS

Four small slices of tofu (approximately 2" x 2" x 1/4" thick)

fried in Pam or other non-stick spray.

1 large egg

1 Tbsp. (rounded) fat free Greek yogurt

1 tsp olive oil

Sea salt and freshly ground black pepper to season

INSTRUCTIONS

1. Preheat oven to 350°F (175°C).
2. Fry the tofu slices in a little of the olive oil and season with some sea salt and freshly ground black pepper.
3. Mix the egg with the yogurt in a bowl adding more seasoning if desired. Grease the inside of a ramekin dish with the remaining oil.

4. Assemble your soufflé starting with a little egg then a layer of tofu. Pour in the rest of the egg mixture and top with a layer of tofu.

5. Cook for around 20 minutes and then check the center using a skewer or toothpick to make sure it is cook through.

6. Remove from dish and serve.

Herby Omelet

Prep time: 5 min

Cook time: Approx. 10 min

Servings: 1

INGREDIENTS

1 whole egg

1 egg white

1 Tbsp. skim milk

Chopped herbs of choice

Salt and pepper

INSTRUCTIONS

1. Beat the egg, egg white and milk in a small bowl.
2. Add a little salt and pepper. Add in your herbs of choice.
3. Heat a pan over a medium heat and add a few drops of oil wipe away with a piece of kitchen paper.
4. Pour the mix into the pan and cook until done.
5. Fold your omelet in half before putting on a plate. Serve hot.

Lunch & Dinner

Chicken Supreme

Prep time: 15 min

Cook time: Approx. 15 min

Servings: 1

INGREDIENTS

1 6-8oz Chicken Breast

1 glass of White Wine (Tolerated)

2 Tbsp. Fat Free Yogurt

1 tsp Chopped Chives

1 tsp Dijon Mustard

Salt and Pepper to taste

INSTRUCTIONS

1. Cut the chicken breast into strips and dry fry in a pan on medium heat for one minute on each side to seal.
2. Add the white wine and cook until the chicken is done.
3. In a bowl mix, the remaining ingredients to make the sauce.
4. Allow the chicken to cool slightly before adding the sauce and then serve.

Tandoori Chicken Recipe

Prep time: 45 min

Cook time: Approx. 15 min

Servings: 2

INGREDIENTS

10-12oz chicken tenders or breasts

1/4 tsp curry powder

1/4 tsp red pepper flakes

1/8 tsp ground ginger

1/8 tsp smoked paprika

1/8 tsp cinnamon

1/8 tsp turmeric

1 Tbsp water

Salt and pepper

Olive oil spray

INSTRUCTIONS

1. In a bowl, mix all spices with water. Mix into a paste until completely smooth.

2. Put the paste on the tenders. Allow to marinate for 30 minutes.

3. In a grill pan sprayed with olive oil spray heat over medium heat. Cook tenders 5-7 minutes per side or until done.

Tequila-Lime Chicken Wings And Thighs

Prep time: 15 min

Cook time: Approx. 70 min

Servings: 2

INGREDIENTS

1/4 cup lime juice

1/8 cup tequila

1/2 Tbsp agave syrup (or 1/2 tsp Splenda)

1/2 tsp lime zest

1/2 tsp ground cumin

1/4 Serrano pepper, finely diced

1 1/2 lbs of skinless chicken wings, thighs, or combination of both

1/2 tsp cornstarch

INSTRUCTIONS

1. Preheat oven to 450.

2. Season the chicken with salt and pepper and bake for 30 minutes.

3. Mix all the sauce ingredients in a bowl and pour the sauce over the chicken and bake for an additional 30 minutes, constantly basting.

4. Drain the sauce into a saucepan and add the cornstarch. Cook for 5 minutes, until thick.

5. Pour over chicken and serve.

Lemon Garlic Chicken Thighs And Tenders

Prep time: 5 min

Cook time: Approx. 45 min

Servings: 2

INGREDIENTS

2 boneless, skinless chicken thighs

4 chicken tenders

1 cup low sodium chicken broth

1 small onion, thinly sliced

8-10 large cloves of garlic, crushed

2 tsp cornstarch

Juice of 1/2 a lemon

1/2 tsp red pepper flakes

INSTRUCTIONS

1. Preheat oven to 350 degrees.
2. Put chicken in a plastic bag. Add salt, pepper, and cornstarch and shake until coated.

3. Spray skillet with cooking spray, and heat on medium. Add chicken to skillet, browning each side. Approx. 7 minutes each side for thighs, and 5 minutes for tenders. After browned, remove from skillet and set to the side.

4. Sauté the onions in the pan for about 5 minutes, add the garlic and red pepper flakes and cook for another minute. Add the lemon juice and broth.

5. Place the chicken back in the pan. Bring to a simmer, cover and bake at 350 degrees for 15 minutes.

6. Remove the cover and cook for another 5-10 minutes, until chicken is fully cooked. Serve with lemon slices.

Salisbury Steak

Prep time: 10 min

Cook time: Approx. 30 min

Servings: 2

INGREDIENTS

1/4 lb ground turkey

1/4 lb ground sirloin

¾ cups water

1/8 cup oat bran

1/2 egg or 1/8 cup egg white substitute

1/4 onion, finely chopped

1 1/2 Tbsp. tomato paste

1 Tbsp. sherry or Madeira wine

½ Tbsp. tomato paste

½ Tbsp. corn starch mixed with ½ Tbsp. water

3/4 tsp Worcestershire sauce

1/4 package dry onion soup mix

INSTRUCTIONS

1. Combine turkey, beef, oat bran, tomato paste, egg and onion in a large bowl and season with salt and pepper.

2. Divide meat into 2-3 portions and form patties. Brown patties over medium heat. Cooking approximately 6 minutes, flipping halfway through.

3. Remove and keep warm on a plate covered with foil.

4. Stir in the tomato paste into skillet and cook for 1 minute.

5. Add the water and the rest of the ingredients and bring to boil. Add patties back into the skillet.

6. Cover and simmer for 10 minutes. Uncover and cook until liquid reduces, about 10 more minutes.

Steak Ranchera

Prep time: 10 min

Cook time: Approx. 10 min

Servings: 2

INGREDIENTS

1 lb thinly sliced sirloin steak

1/2 onion, sliced

1/2 red bell pepper

1/2 bunch cilantro

INSTRUCTIONS

1. Preheat grill pan on medium high heat.
2. Add bell peppers, onions, and steak slices to skillet until done. Approx. 3 minutes per side.
3. Add the cilantro to skillet and just wilt the leaves.
4. Serve steak with wilted cilantro, your choice of vegetables, and ranchera salsa.

Ranchera Salsa

Prep time: 15 min

Cook time: Approx. 20 min

Servings: 2

INGREDIENTS

12 small tomatillos, washed, husked and cut in half

2 Tbsp. tomato paste

1 Tbsp. paprika

½ cup water

1/3 cup cilantro, chopped

2 cloves of garlic, finely chopped

½ small onion, finely chopped

1 jalapeno, seeded and finely chopped

1 drop, liquid smoke (optional)

¼ tsp cayenne pepper

¼ tsp ancho chili powder

¼ tsp chili powder

salt and pepper

INSTRUCTIONS

1. Heat a skillet on medium heat. Add garlic and tomatillos. Roast together about 15 minutes until they are soft.

2. Put the tomatillos mixture, garlic, cilantro, tomato paste, liquid smoke and water in a blender or food processor until smooth.

3. Add seasonings, including salt and pepper.

4. Add the onion once the salsa is finished. Hand mix to fold in salsa.

Rosemary Beef Burgers With Dill And Paprika Dip

Prep time: 10 min

Cook time: Approx. 15 min

Servings: 2

INGREDIENTS

For the burgers:

50g lean beef mince

¼ whole egg

1 Tbsp. of oat bran if you're in the Cruise Phase, 3 if you're on Attack

¼ tsp of chopped fresh rosemary

¼ tsp of nutmeg

freshly ground black pepper

For the dip:

50g of 0% fat Greek yogurt

¼ tsp of smoked paprika

½ tsp of dried dill

INSTRUCTIONS

1. Prepare the yogurt dip by mixing all the ingredients in a bowl, cover with cling film and pop in the fridge.

2. To make the burgers, mix all the ingredients listen above in a food processor. After mix in a bowl using a fork to make sure all is mixed well.

3. Divide the mixture into 2 portions and use your hands to shape them into small burgers.

4. Heat up a griddle pan over high heat for about 5 minutes until very hot. Place the burgers on the griddle pan and cook until the meat is cooked through and the burgers are browned.

5. Serve hot with the dill and paprika dip on PP days or combine with a healthy green salad on P+V days.

Crispy Chicken Kebabs

Prep time: 10 min

Cook time: Approx. 25 min

Servings: 2 (approx. 4 pieces each serving)

INGREDIENTS

50ml (2floz) soy sauce

1.5 garlic cloves (less if you prefer), diced and cut finely

1-2 Tbsp. of sweetener (liquid or powder if dissolved in a touch of water)

3 Tbsp. of 5 spice powder

Pinch of chopped ginger

Pinch of salt and pepper

1/4 of chick stock cube

Paprika

8 Chicken Wings with skins removed

INSTRUCTIONS

1. Place all ingredients in a bowl, allowing the chicken to marinate for a minimum of 3-4 hours, but overnight would be ideal.

2. Make sure to mix or turn them a few times while marinating.

3. Once ready place in an aluminum tin and cook on the grill until done. Approximately 12 minutes, when done you will hear the chicken sizzle.

4. Flip to over side to brown, approximately another 8 minutes. Making sure both sides are browned. Serve hot.

Spinach Fettuccini Shirataki with Ground Beef

Prep time: 5 min

Cook time: Approx. 20 min

Servings: 2

INGREDIENTS

2 packs Dukan Diet Spinach Fettuccini Shirataki

1 pound lean grass-fed ground beef

½ cup parsley, chopped

Pepper to taste

INSTRUCTIONS

1. Prepare Shirataki noodles as per package instructions and set aside.
2. Sautee ground beef in a pan with pepper over medium heat, about 5-8 minutes.
3. Add parsley and noodles and cook for another 5 minutes. Plate and serve.

Turkey Shirataki

Prep time: 5 min

Cook time: Approx. 20 min

Servings: 2

INGREDIENTS

2 pouches of Dukan Diet Shirataki Noodles

1 lb. ground lean turkey breast

1 Tbsp. Cumin

1 Tbsp. Coriander

1 Tbsp. Fennel seeds

¼ Tsp. Black pepper

1 stalk green onion (optional)

INSTRUCTIONS

1. Sauté ground turkey in a skillet over medium heat.
2. Add the coriander, fennel, cumin, and black pepper.
3. Prepare noodles per the package instructions. Add to the turkey mixture.
4. Toss well and serve.

Caraway Flavored Pork Chops

Prep time: 10 min

Cook time: Approx. 25 min

Servings: 1

INGREDIENTS

2 pork chops

1 lemon

1 Tbsp. caraway seeds

Salt and pepper

INSTRUCTIONS

1. Heat the oven to 180C degrees.
2. Place the pork chops on a chopping board, remove all visible fat and place pork chop on the plate.
3. Using a pestle and mortar, grind the caraway seeds into a powder, rub all over the pork chops and season with salt and pepper.
4. Sear the meat by frying it on medium heat in a non-stick pan which has previously been greased slightly.

5. When the meat is starting to brown, transfer the pork chops to a roasting tin and roast in the oven until the meat is cooked through.

6. Squeeze the lemon juice on the pork chops, plate and serve hot.

Oat Bran Galette Sandwich

Prep time: 10 min

Cook time: Approx. 10 min

Servings: 1

INGREDIENTS

For the oat bran galette:

2 whole eggs or egg whites (if you suffer of cholesterol problems)

3 Tbsp. oat bran

3 Tbsp. 0% fat Greek yoghurt

Your favorite herbs or spices

For the filling:

6 oz Lean cooked meats (beef, ham, turkey, turkey ham, chicken all work very well)

2 Tbsp. low fat cream cheese

INSTRUCTIONS

1. Prepare the oat bran galette following our basic recipe and flavor the pancake batter with spices or herbs of your liking before cooking. Once ready, set aside to cool.

2. Cut the galette in half and spread a generous layer of cream cheese on each side, just like you would if you were using bread.

3. Fill your sandwich with your preferred cooked meat and, voilà, you have a yummy Dukan-friendly sarnie to enjoy!

Dukan Beef Tataki

Prep time: 15 min

Cook time: Approx. 15 min

Servings: 2

INGREDIENTS

1 lb of trimmed boneless sirloin steak about 1 inch thick

1 cup of radishes or peeled daikon radish cut into matchstick batons

1 cup of carrots cut into matchstick batons

1 large thinly sliced onion

4 Tbsp. soy sauce

3 Tbsp. lemon juice

2 Tbsp. finely chopped scallions/spring onions

2 tsp finely grated fresh ginger

2 tsp of rapeseed oil

Sea salt and freshly ground black pepper

INSTRUCTIONS

1. Put the sliced onion and carrot and radish batons in a bowl and cover with very cold water for 5 minutes and then drain.
2. Mix together the soy sauce, ginger, scallions, lemon juice in a bowl.
3. Add 2 tablespoons of the seasoning mixture to the vegetables, tossing well to completely cover them. Keeping the remaining sauce to use later.
4. Season both sides of steak with salt and pepper.
5. Heat oil in a large nonstick pan on a medium-high heat.
6. Fry the steak for 3 to 4 minutes each side and then allow to rest for about 5 minutes before slicing very thinly.
7. Arrange the meat slices on top of the salad and drizzle with the remaining sauce. Serve hot.

Oriental Style Braised Beef

Prep time: 10 min

Cook time: Approx. 1 hour 45 min

Servings: 2-3

INGREDIENTS

750 g of lean braising beef

3 Tbsp. dark soy sauce

2 Tbsp. corn flour

1 Tbsp. grated fresh ginger

1 finely sliced onion

4 cloves of finely sliced garlic

1 deseeded and finely chopped red chili

4 tsp rapeseed oil

1 tsp Chinese five-spice powder

500 ml of water

Sweetener to taste

1 Tbsp. fresh chopped cilantro/coriander

INSTRUCTIONS

1. Cut the beef into chunks and toss in a bowl with the corn flour to coat.
2. Heat two teaspoons of oil in a pot and brown the meat over medium high heat.
3. Remove the meat and add the remaining two teaspoons of oil. Cook the onion, garlic, ginger and chili until soft.
4. Add the browned meat and teaspoon of Chinese five-spice powder and cook for a further five minutes.
5. Add the water, soy sauce and sweetener and bring to a slow steady simmer.
6. Cook until the meat is really tender which should be about 90 minutes.
7. Stir in the chopped cilantro/coriander just before serving.

Egg and Onion Bhurji

Prep time: 10 min

Cook time: Approx. 25 min

Servings: 2

INGREDIENTS

4 eggs

2 Tbsp. of fat free milk

1 diced medium onion

2 crushed cloves of garlic

2 finely diced green chilies

2 tsp tomato puree

1/2 tsp turmeric

1/2 tsp masala or curry powder

2 tsp rapeseed oil

1 Tbsp. chopped cilantro/coriander to garnish

INSTRUCTIONS

1. Beat the eggs and milk in a bowl. Preheat skillet to medium heat, adding oil.

2. In the skillet, add the onion, garlic and chilies in the oil until the onion is soft.

3. Add the tomato puree, turmeric and masala/curry powder and cook for a further 2/3 minutes.

4. Add the egg mixture and stir until the eggs are cooked to the consistency you prefer.

5. Serve immediately garnished with the chopped cilantro/coriander.

Salmon in Wasabi Sauce

Prep time: 25 min

Cook time: Approx. 25 min

Servings: 2

INGREDIENTS

2 pieces of salmon fillet

2 tsp rapeseed oil

2 scallions/spring onions

1 cloves of garlic

½ small bunch of fresh cilantro/coriander

2 Tbsp. fat free Greek yogurt

3 Tbsp. lemon juice sweetened to taste with sweetener

Salt and pepper to taste

½ Tbsp. of "wasabi" paste

INSTRUCTIONS

1. Peel and finely chop the garlic. Then wash and chop the cilantro/coriander, keeping back a few leaves to garnish the finished dish.

2. Wash the scallions/spring onions and finely slice.

3. Season the fish with salt and pepper.

4. Heat oil in a non-stick pan and fry the salmon at a medium heat on each side for approximately 5 minutes.

5. Add garlic and spring onions to the salmon and sauté for 2 minutes.

6. Remove the salmon from the pan and keep warm on a serving dish.

7. In a bowl mix, the yogurt with two tablespoons of sweetened lemon juice until smooth. Add the remaining sweetened lemon juice and allow to cool slightly before stirring in the yogurt.

8. Add the wasabi paste and dissolving in the sauce before stirring in the chopped cilantro/coriander.

9. Pour the sauce over the salmon fillets and garnish before serving.

Turkey Meatloaf

Prep time: 10 min

Cook time: Approx. 25 min

Servings: 2

INGREDIENTS

16 oz ground Turkey (Turkey Mince)

4 Tbsp. Oat Bran

1 finely diced medium-sized Onion

2 Tbsp. Balsamic Vinegar

1 tsp Paprika

1 tsp Cayenne Pepper

2 Egg Whites

Sea Salt and Freshly Ground Black Pepper to taste.

INSTRUCTIONS

1. Preheat oven to 350 F, 180 C or Gas Mark 4
2. Mix your paprika and cayenne pepper with the oat bran in a large bowl with a little salt and black pepper.
3. Add the turkey and onion, mix well.

4. Add in the egg whites and balsamic vinegar and work into the meat.

5. You should be able to form the mixture without it coming apart. If the mixture is too wet you can add a little more oat bran or some wheat bran. If the mixture is too dry you could add a little fat free yogurt to moisten.

6. Separate meat mixture into two. Form your meatloaf on a non-stick baking sheet or use a muffin tray to make mini meatloafs.

7. Place in a preheated oven for up to 45 minutes. The time needed will vary according to the shape and size of your meatloafs.

Lemon Zesty Grilled Calamari with Garlic

Prep time: 2 hours 10 min

Cook time: Approx. 10 min

Servings: 2

INGREDIENTS

2 (8oz) Squid-cleaned, rinsed and dried with kitchen paper

1 lemon, juice and zest

1 tsp Olive Oil

1 clove garlic, finely diced

Sea Salt and freshly ground Black Pepper

Fresh chopped Coriander/Cilantro/coriander to garnish

1 lemon cut into quarters to garnish

INSTRUCTIONS

1. Cut the squid open by slicing down the side of the tube.
2. Carefully score the inside of the flesh in a diamond pattern making sure not to cut all the way through.

3. In a bowl mix the lemon juice, lemon zest, garlic, olive oil and salt and pepper.

4. Rub the marinade into the squid, cover the bowl with cling film and leave to marinate for at least two hours in the refrigerator.

5. Heat your barbecue or griddle until hot. Place the squid on the heat for about two minutes each side.

6. Serve on a plate garnished with the fresh chopped cilantro/coriander and a lemon quarter.

7. Squeeze the lemon juice on the squid just before eating.

Pan Fried Trout with Lemon & Bay Leaf

Prep time: 25 min

Cook time: Approx. 15 min

Servings: 1

INGREDIENTS

1 Trout

1 Lemon

1 Bay leaf

A little salt and pepper

INSTRUCTIONS

1. Clean and gut your trout but leave it whole, removing the head if preferred.
2. Cut three slices from the middle of the lemon and put them to one side. Squeeze the lemon juice from the remaining parts of the lemon into the cavity and over the fish.

3. Cut one lemon slice in half and place both halves in the cavity of the fish with the bay leaf.

4. Season with a little salt and pepper and dry fry in a pan until cooked through, turning half way.

5. Use the remaining slices of lemon as a garnish when serving.

Snacks & Appetizers

Cinnamon Oat Bran Muffins

Prep time: 10 min

Cook time: Approx. 20 min

Servings: 6 (1 muffins per serving)

INGREDIENTS

2 eggs

6 Tbsp. zero fat yogurt

6 Tbsp. oat bran

1 ½ tsp cinnamon

1 tsp of baking powder

Sweetener to taste

INSTRUCTIONS

1. Preheat oven to 350 degrees.
2. Add all the dry ingredients into a bowl, mixing them together well.
3. Add the eggs and yogurt, whisking until mixture is smooth. Once smooth, add sweetener to your preference.

4. Place 6 paper muffin wraps in a muffin tray. Separate the mixture equally between 6 paper muffin wraps. Bake for 15-18 minutes.

Israeli-Spiced Meatballs

Prep time: 10 min

Cook time: Approx. 30 min

Servings: 2

INGREDIENTS

½ lb ground turkey

¼ cup fat free cottage cheese

¼ cup Pistachio Spice Mix

1/8 cup oat bran

½ egg, beaten with fork

1 tsp Harisa

½ tsp Hot Paprika

INSTRUCTIONS

1. Preheat oven to 400 degrees.
2. Mix all ingredients except for Harisa. Do not over mix!
3. Spray a foiled cookie sheet with a dash of cooking spray. Form 8-10 medium meatballs and place on sheet.
4. Bake for 15 minutes.

5. Once removed from oven, top each meatball with a touch of Harisa. Return cookie sheet to over to cook an additional 10-15 minute.

Dukan Coffee Frappuccino

Prep time: 5 min

Cook time: Approx. 0 min

Servings: 2

INGREDIENTS

1 cup of strong black coffee or espresso, cold

1 cup of skimmed milk straight from the fridge

4 tsp aspartame

16 ice cubes

INSTRUCTIONS

1. Put the coffee, milk and sweetener into a blender and blend until the mixture has become nice and foamy.
2. Add the ice and blend until the ice has broken up into small pieces.
3. Stir well, split into two tall glasses to serve.

Herb-Sauteed Shrimp

Prep time: 5 min

Cook time: Approx. 10 min

Servings: 2

INGREDIENTS

1lb shrimps, peeled, de-veined and rinsed

2 garlic cloves, crushed

15g (1/2 oz) fresh parsley, chopped

25ml (1fl oz) dry white wine

1 lemon, cut in half

INSTRUCTIONS

1. Preheat non-stick skillet to medium heat.
2. Add the shrimps, garlic, parsley and wine.
3. Sauté until the shrimps are pink.
4. Serve with fresh lemon.

Meatball Stuffed Mushrooms

Prep time: 10 min

Cook time: Approx. 25 min

Servings: 1-2

INGREDIENTS

8 medium mushrooms, stems removed

½ lb ground turkey

½ egg, mixed with a fork

¼ cup fat free mozzarella cheese

¼ cup fat free cottage cheese

1/8 cup oat bran

1/8 cup fresh basil, chopped

1 Tbsp tomato paste

1 Tbsp Parmesan cheese

Salt and pepper

INSTRUCTIONS

1. Preheat oven to 425

2. In a bowl, mix all ingredients except mushrooms and salt and pepper, careful not to handle too much.

3. Season with salt and pepper. Spoon 2 Tbsp. of meat mixture, into the mushrooms.

4. If you have leftover you can always just make extra meatballs for lunch tomorrow!

5. Bake for 20-25 minutes.

Chicken Breast Wrapped in Turkey Bacon

Prep time: 15 min

Cook time: Approx. 30 min

Servings: 2

INGREDIENTS

2 chicken breast fillets (skin removed)

4 turkey back rashers

4 Tbsp. Quark, heaped

Handful of chopped chives

Freshly ground black pepper

INSTRUCTIONS

1. Preheat oven to 375 degrees.
2. Take the 2 chicken breast fillets and slice halfway through the chicken to create pockets for filling.
3. Season the chicken breast fillets with freshly ground black pepper and set aside.

4. In a small ramekin or bowl, mix together the Quark and the chopped chives. Spoon half of the mixture into each chicken breast fillet.

5. Wrap each chicken breast fillet with 2 rashers of turkey bacon, this will keep the chicken succulent and add an extra layer of flavor.

6. Bake each chicken breasts for approximately 25 - 30 minutes, or until the chicken is cooked the whole way through and juices run clear.

7. Serve straight out of the oven while the bacon is still crispy!

Stuffed Eggs with Shrimps/Prawns

Prep time: 10 min

Cook time: Approx. 25 min

Servings: 2 (2 halves per serving)

INGREDIENTS

2 hardboiled eggs

80g shrimps/prawns, rinsed cleaned, cooked and chopped

Dukan recipe oil free mayo

Paprika or Red Chili to garnish

INSTRUCTIONS

1. Cut each egg into two equal parts (oblong). Removing the yolks.
2. Smash the yolks until no large chunks remain then mix in the cooked shrimp/prawns.
3. Stir in mayo and mix well until mixture is smooth.
4. Spoon in the mixture into cooled egg white halves.

5. Sprinkle with crushed red chili or a dash of paprika to garnish and for extra flavor.

Dukan Prawn Cocktail

Prep time: 10 min

Cook time: Approx. 60 min (to chill)

Servings: 2-3

INGREDIENTS

150g cooked cocktail prawns

200g 0% fat Greek yogurt

1 Tbsp. chopped chives

A pinch of paprika

A squeeze of lemon juice

Tabasco sauce, optional

INSTRUCTIONS

1. Place the Greek yogurt in a bowl and fold in the paprika, chives, lemon juice, and tabasco sauce.

2. Mix well until all ingredients have blended together. Add the prawns and mix until they are nicely covered with the sauce.

3. Garnish with a sprinkle of paprika. Chill approx. 60 minutes to serve very cold.

Winter Warming Eggnog

Prep time: 5 min

Cook time: Approx. 1-2 min

Servings: 1

INGREDIENTS

225ml of skim/skimmed milk

1 egg yolk

2 tsp Splenda or other sweetener of your choice

A few drops of vanilla essence

Nutmeg and cinnamon to taste

INSTRUCTIONS

1. In a microwaveable mug, heat milk on high for about 60 seconds.
2. In a small bowl beat the egg yolk and Splenda until creamy.
3. Slowly add the milk and stir well until combined.
4. Add the vanilla essence and pour back into your mug.
5. Top with a dusting of nutmeg and cinnamon.

Oat Bran Free Dukan Diet Rolls

Prep time: 15 min

Cook time: Approx. 40 min

Servings: 1

INGREDIENTS

1 eggs

1 Tbsp. cottage cheese (2% fat) or Fat free cream cheese

1/3 tsp sweetener

1/8 tsp cream of tartar

Pam Spray

INSTRUCTIONS

1. Preheat oven to 300°F, 150°C.
2. Separate the eggs very carefully making sure none of the yolk gets into the whites. Beat egg whites with cream of tartar until whites are stiff and stay in the bowl when tipped.
3. Blend the yolks, cottage cheese/cream cheese and sweetener and gently fold into the egg whites taking care not to break down the egg whites.

4. Spray Pam on a Teflon cookie sheet. Place the mixture carefully on the cookie sheet, gently putting one tablespoon full on top of another until each "roll" is about 2 inches high. Repeat this until you have 6 piles.

5. Place the cookie sheet in the oven and bake for about 30 – 40 minutes.

47869352R00050

Made in the USA
San Bernardino, CA
10 April 2017